William Bolcom

Fourth Sonata
for Violin and Piano

I. Allegro brillante

II. White Night

III. Arabesque

IV. Jota

*Commissioned in celebration of the fiftieth
birthday of Henry Rubin by his wife Cynthia.*

Duration: *ca.* 14 minutes

ISBN 0-634-00107-8

EDWARD B. MARKS MUSIC COMPANY / EXCLUSIVELY DISTRIBUTED BY HAL•LEONARD® CORPORATION

7777 W. BLUEMOUND RD. P.O. BOX 13819 MILWAUKEE, WI 53213

Commissioned in celebration of the fiftieth
birthday of Henry Rubin by his wife Cynthia

Fourth Sonata
for Violin and Piano

I

Allegro brillante

William Bolcom (1994)

a tempo

non legato

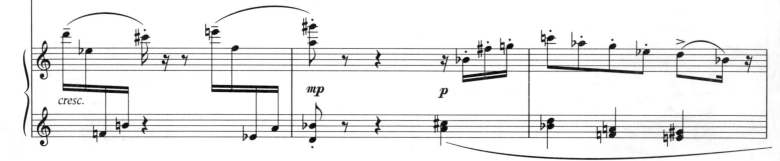

poco slentando

off string

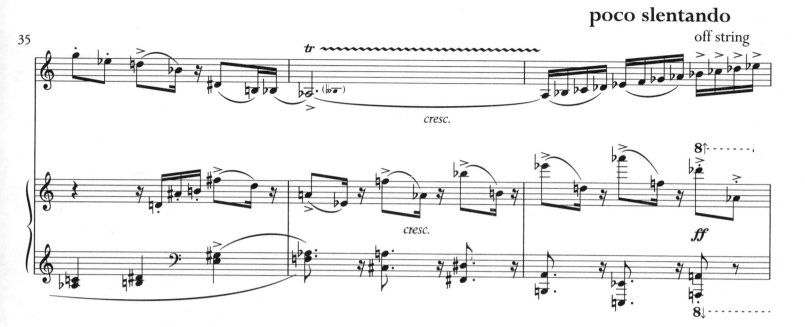

a tempo

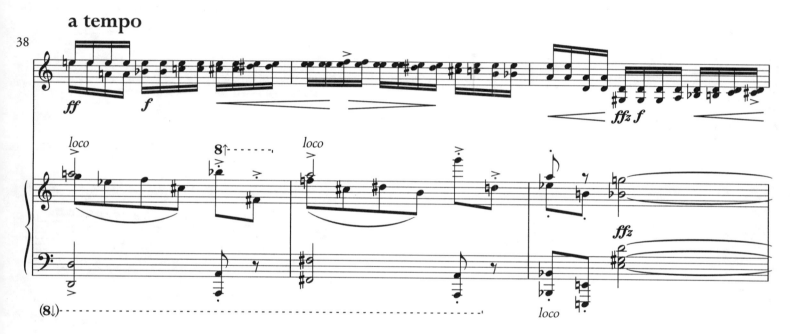

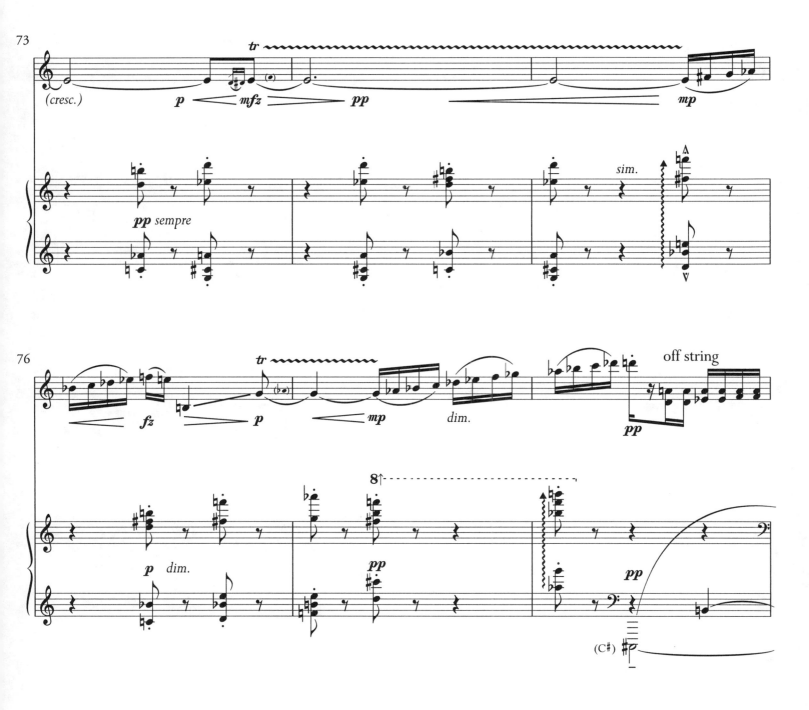

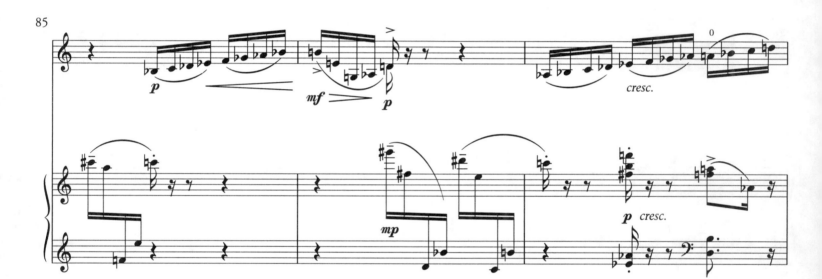

poco slent.   a tempo

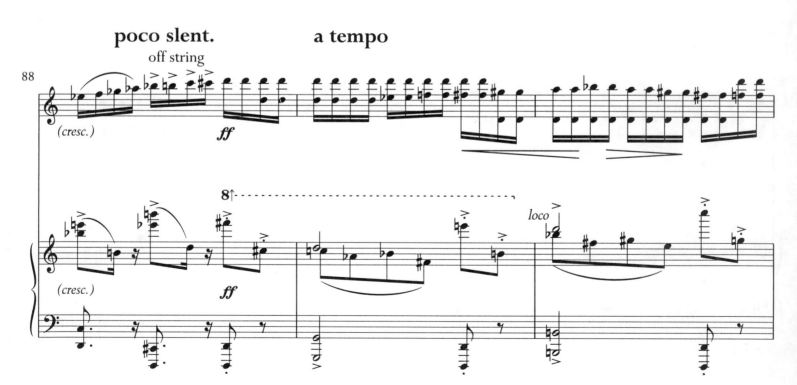

relax
tempo

a tempo

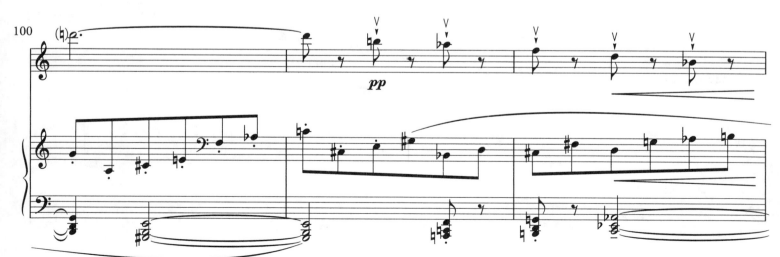

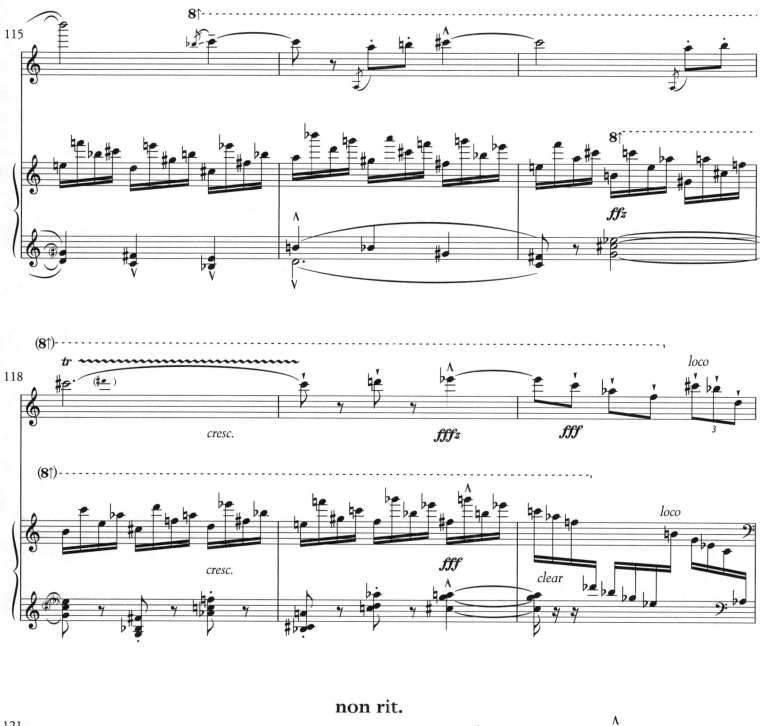

8/30/94 Ann Arbor

segue

II
White Night

*A fitful sleeper recalls an early tune, hoping it will
soothe him to sleep. Instead, it keeps him awake.*

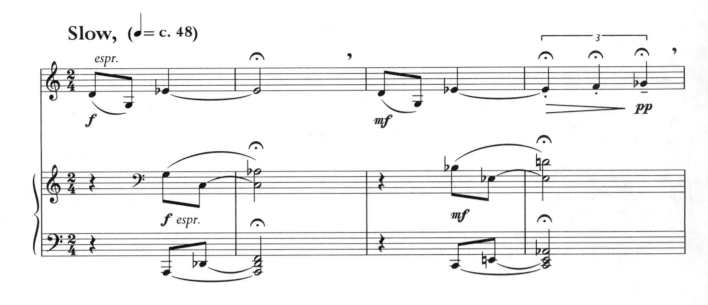

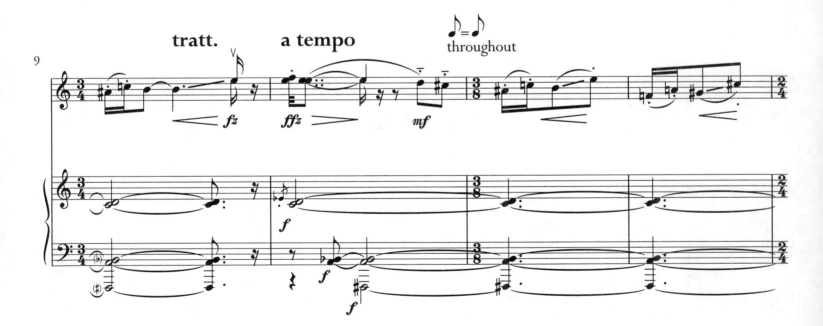

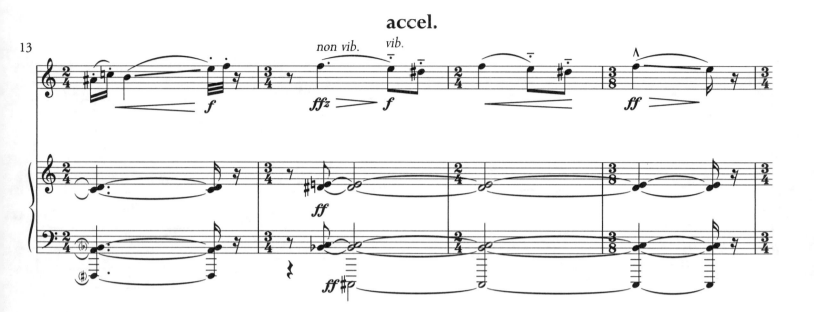

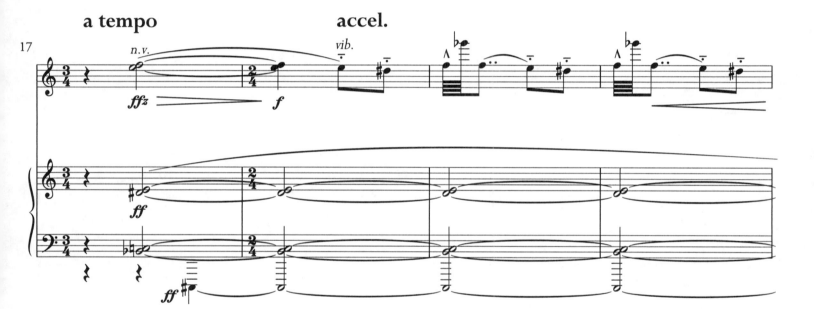

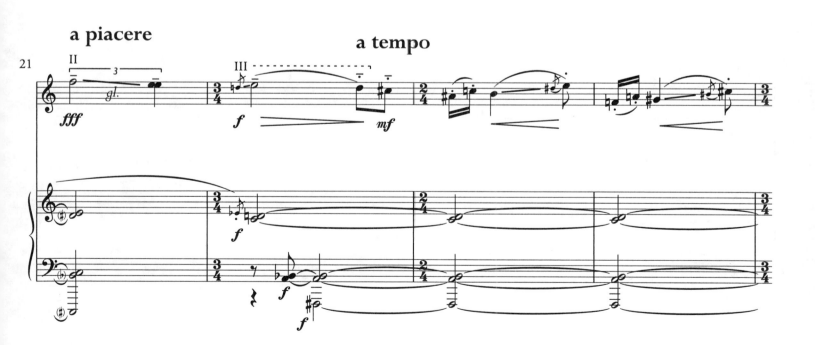

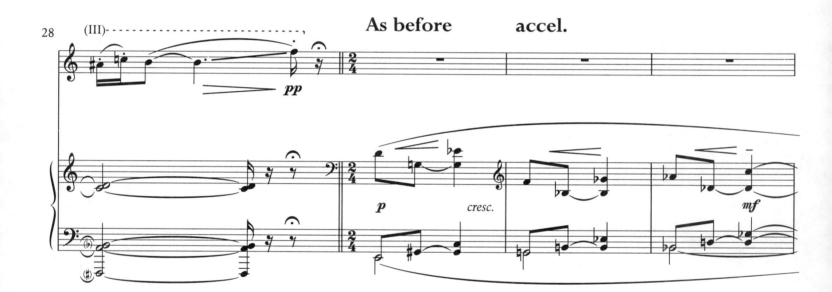

a tempo

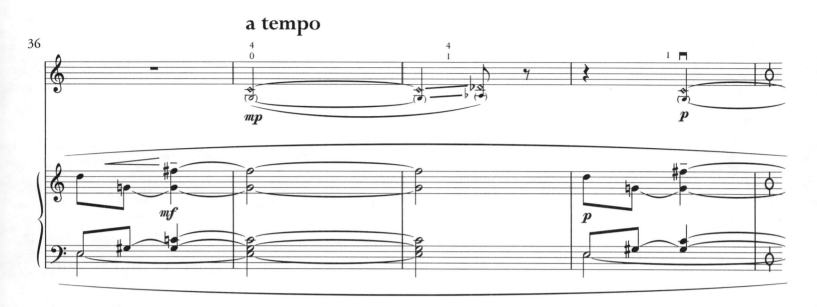

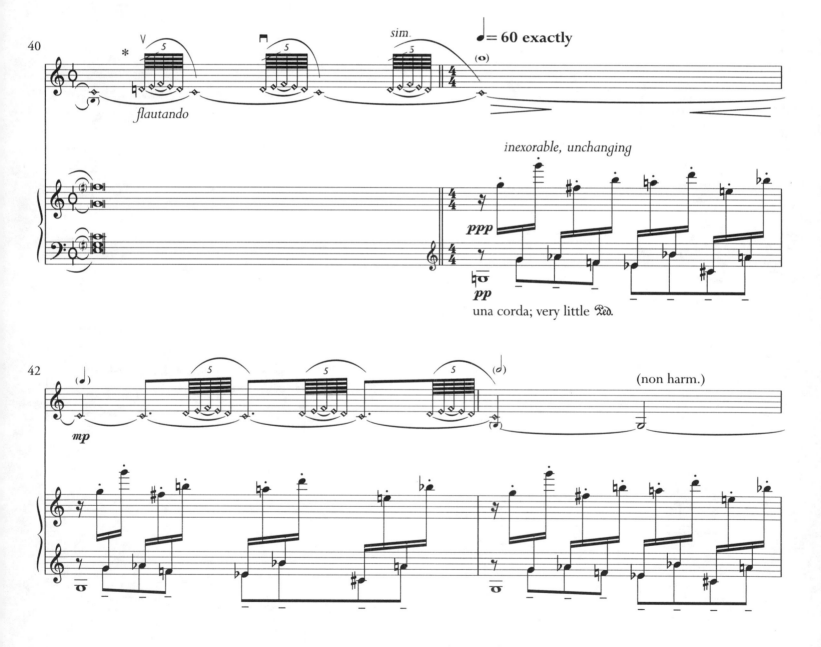

* While holding the lightly-touched C, touch D,
E, and F, also lightly. Do not release the C. Sounds:

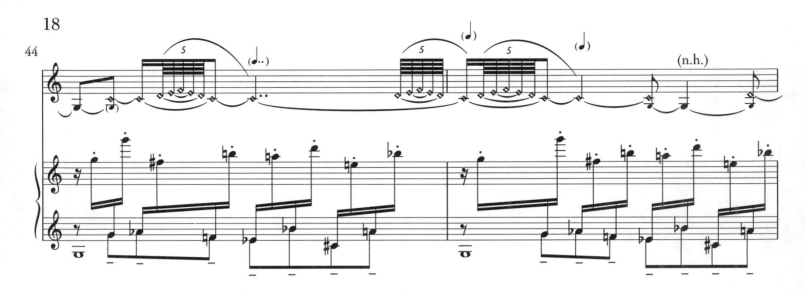

Grazioso, flowing and flexible
(♩ = c. 72+)

rit.

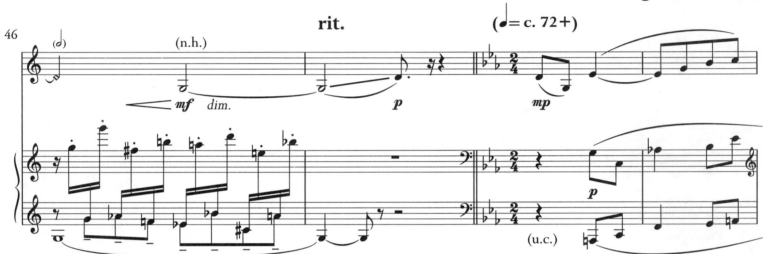

poco rit.

a tempo

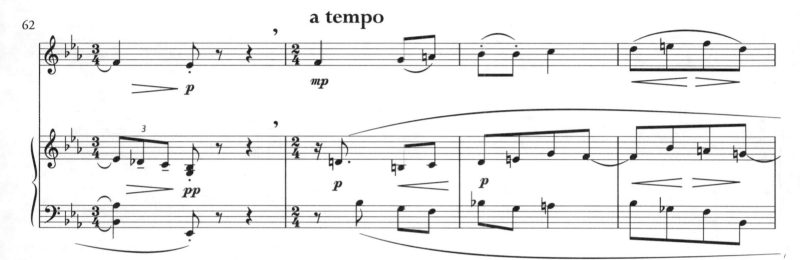

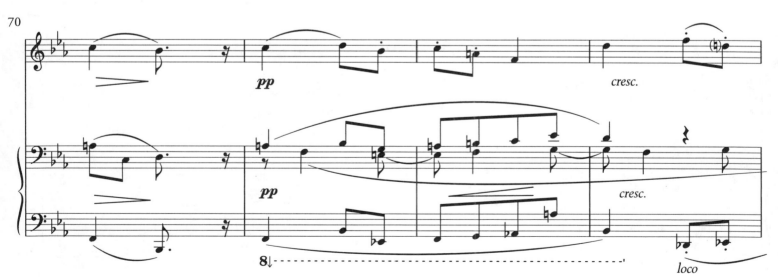

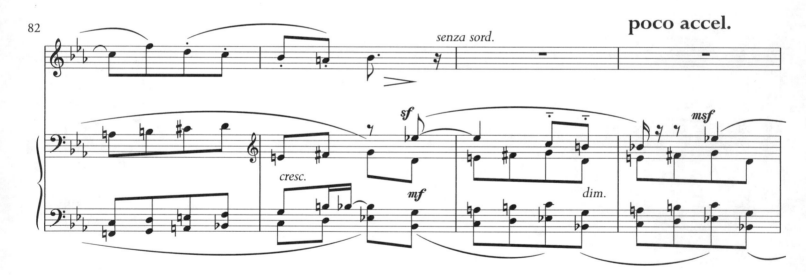

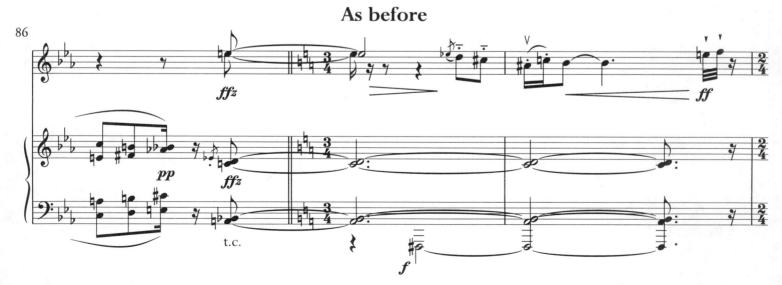

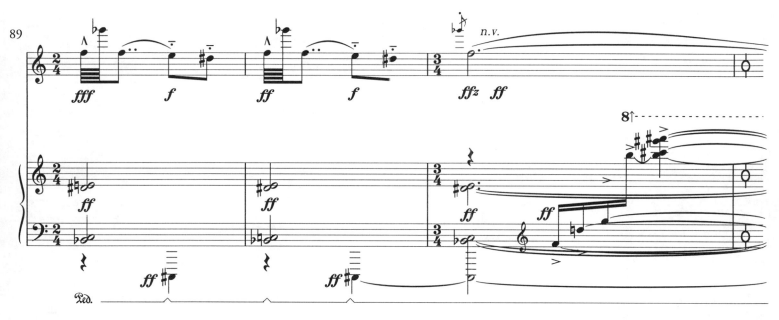

molto accel.   **As before**

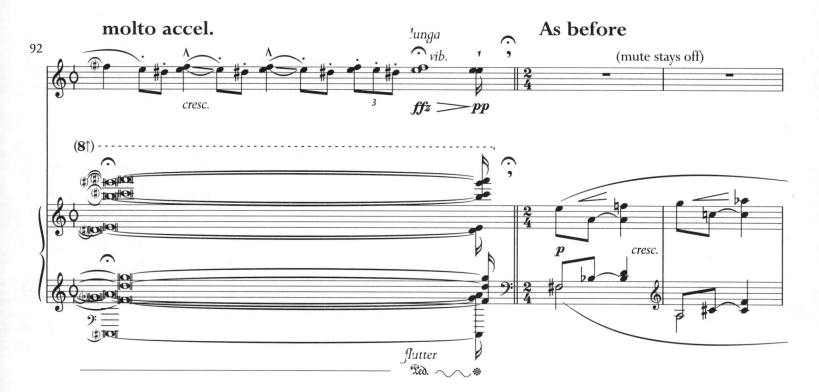

$\quad$=60, as before

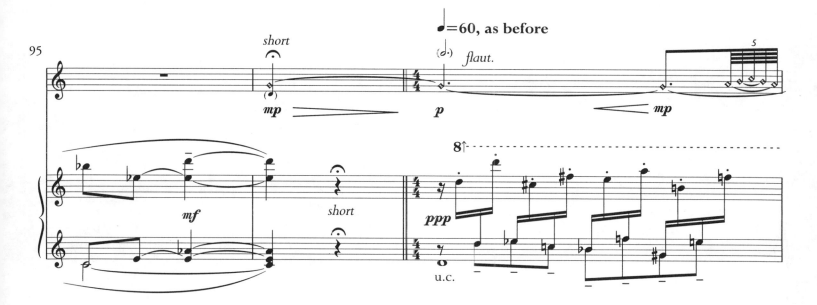

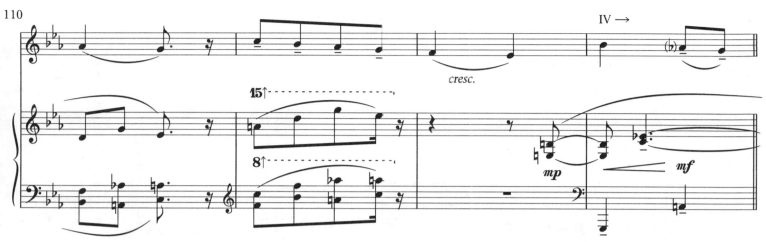

9/4/94 Ann Arbor

III
Arabesque

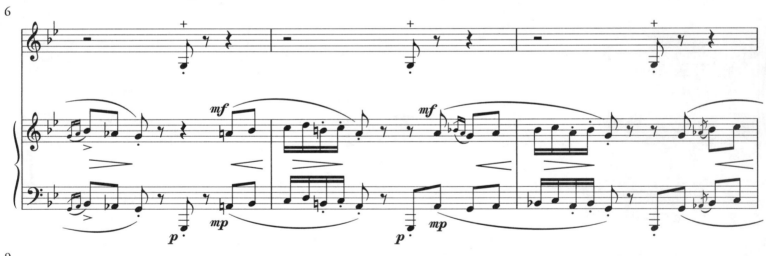

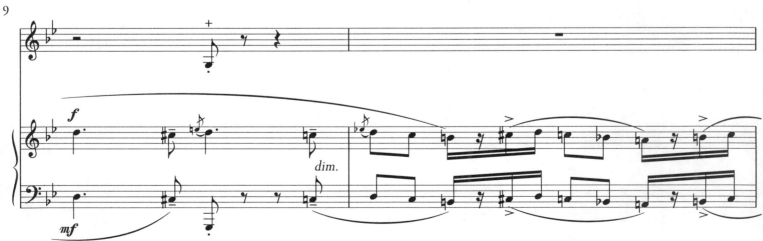

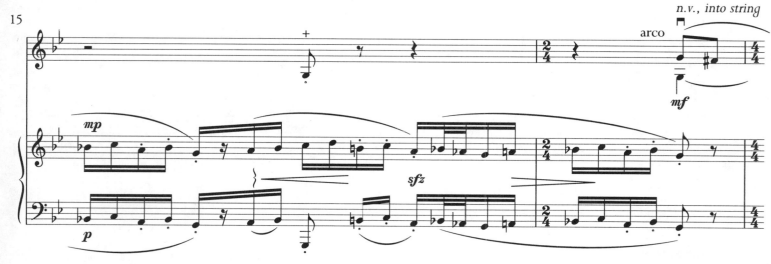

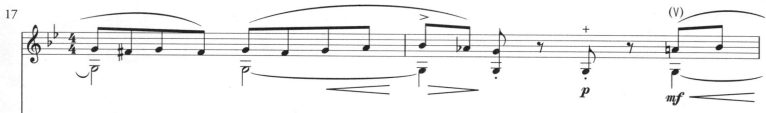

no *Ped.*, very even

* On a Bösendorfer play: through end of passage, m. 30

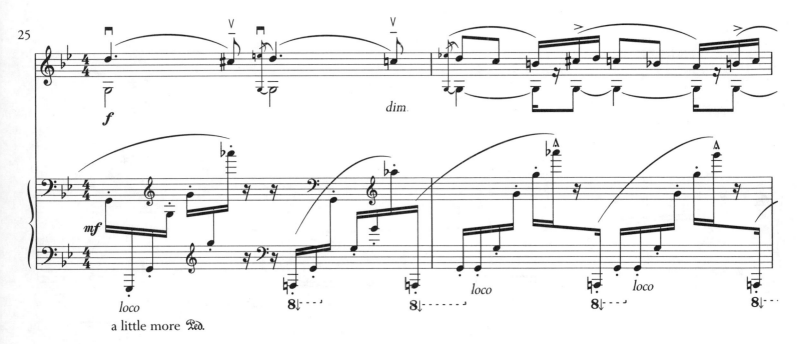

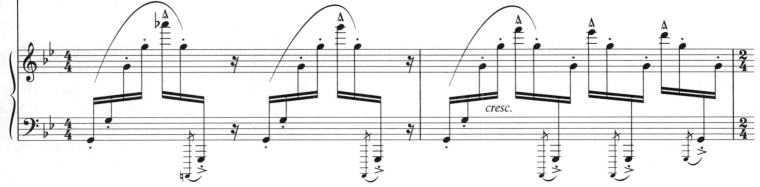

attacca IV

IV
Jota

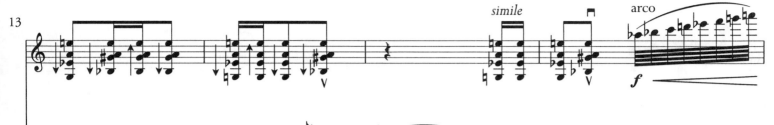

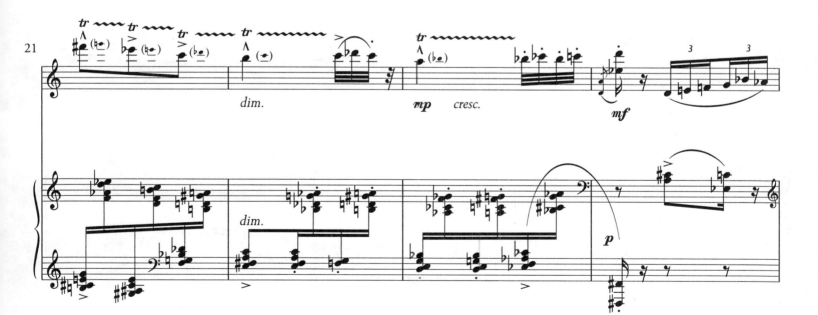

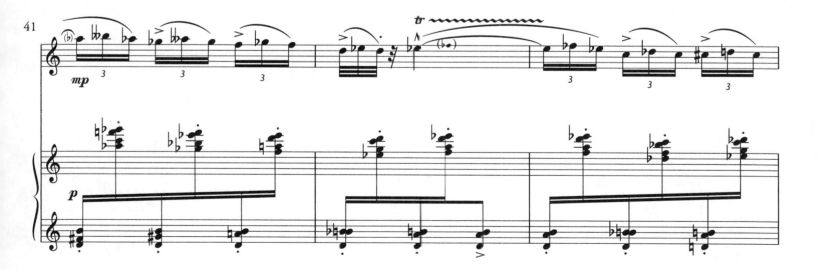

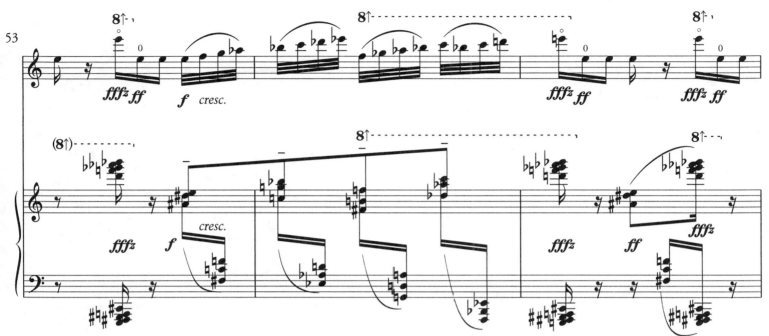

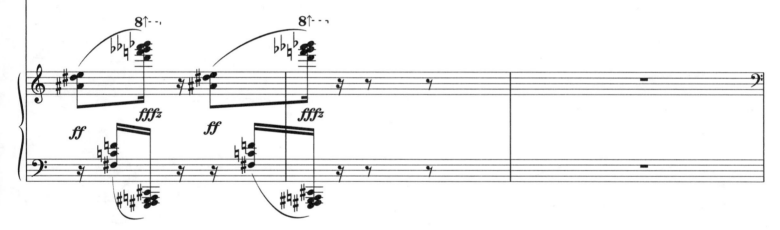

rit. poco a poco

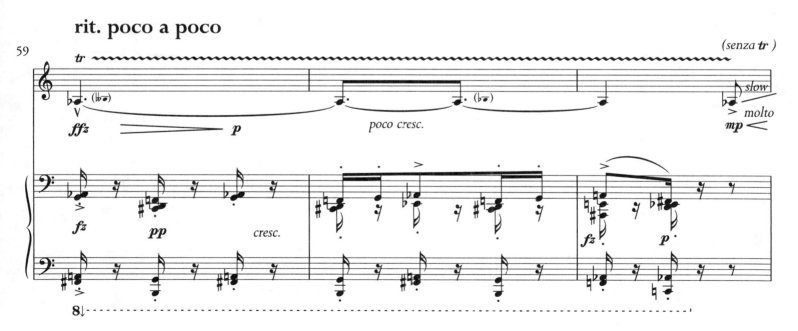

Much slower, rubato

♪=76

(rit.)

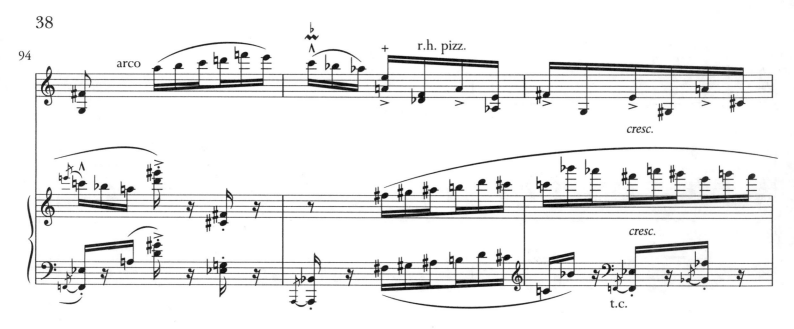

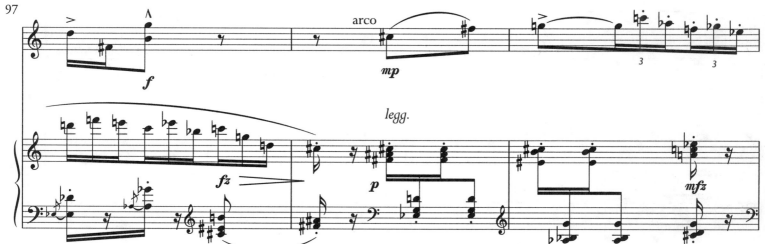

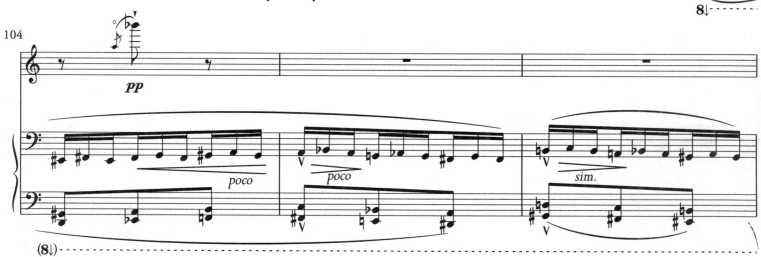

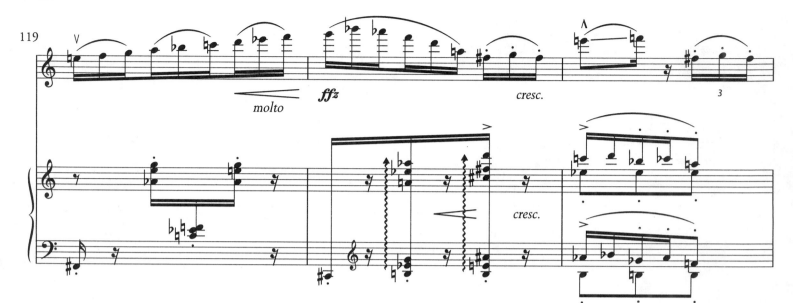

stringendo

molto allarg.

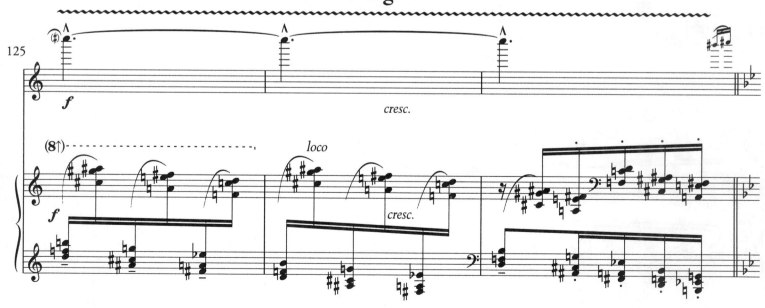

Fateful ♪=112

accel.

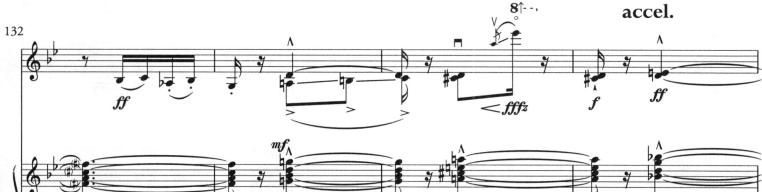

G.P.
(in time)

* On a Bösendorfer play: ** The same: here and in m. 133 & 135

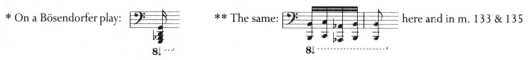

10/29/94 Ann Arbor

NOTE

The *Fourth Sonata for Violin and Piano* was a surprise birthday gift to violinist Henry Rubin, of the University of Houston faculty, from his violinist wife, Cynthia Birdgenaw. Several years ago Ms. Birdgenaw was concertmistress of the University of Michigan Symphony Orchestra.

The premiere of this sonata was given by Mr. Rubin on January 26, 1997, at the University of Michigan in Ann Arbor, with the composer at the piano, in a program of all of Mr. Bolcom's violin sonatas.

NB = 1. In music without a key signature, accidentals apply only throughout a beamed group. In music with a key signature, traditional rules are in force.

2. There are slight differences between the violinist's part and that part in the score. What is in the score represents the composer's intentions; he approves, with thanks, the editorial suggestions appearing in the violinist's part from Professor Henry Rubin, School of Music, University of Houston.